The Veteran

Created by
Amber Guymer-Hosking

HEALING WITH WORD

We Will Remember Them

Published By
Film Volt Group
Company Number
11833932

For the Fallen

BY LAURENCE BINYON

With proud thanksgiving, a mother for her children, England mourns for her
dead across the sea.
Flesh of her flesh they were, spirit of her spirit,
Fallen in the cause of the free.

Solemn the drums thrill; Death august and royal
Sings sorrow up into immortal spheres,
There is music in the midst of desolation
And a glory that shines upon our tears.

They went with songs to the battle, they were young, Straight of limb, true of
eye, steady and aglow.
They were staunch to the end against odds uncounted; They fell with their faces
to the foe.

**They shall grow not old, as we that are left grow old: Age shall not weary
them, nor the years condemn.
At the going down of the sun and in the morning
We will remember them.**

They mingle not with their laughing comrades again; They sit no more at
familiar tables of home;
They have no lot in our labour of the day-time;
They sleep beyond England's foam.

But where our desires are and our hopes profound,
Felt as a well-spring that is hidden from sight,
To the innermost heart of their own land they are known As the stars are known
to the Night;

As the stars that shall be bright when we are dust, Moving in marches upon the
heavenly plain;
As the stars that are starry in the time of our darkness, To the end, to the end,
they remain.

Contents

<u>Special Thanks</u>

I would like to thank all of my siblings for their continued support through my bad and good days. James, Johnny, Miles, Georgina and my son Brandon and my Nephew Charles Henry you're all my heroes. Thank you to my Mother, Grandparents for their continued support.

Thank you to all my family for being here for me on all occasions and fully supporting me in my endeavors and being my confidantes. And to many friends who have been amazing throughout my journey.

I would like to give my thanks to a wonderful charity, that supported me and my son through Homelessness because, without them, I would not be here now.

Help4HomelessVeterans Charity. Tom Wood and his beautiful wife Jean the founders and Steven Bentham-Bates their CEO, along with all of the other colleagues of Help4HomelessVeterans - you are all earth angels and deserve absolute credit for helping Veterans find safety and stability in a home.

I would like to thank you for making me one of your Ambassadors.

I am privileged to be an Ambassador of such a wonderful cause.

Along with a massive thank you for giving me your continued support for the last five years and a lifelong friendship.

I would also like to thank Kate Blewett for the support and opportunities she has given Brandon and me and is now a lifelong friend.

I would also like to give a massive thank you to Mark Busby for creating the front cover, but also for the opportunity and continued support he has given me throughout the last year and your friendship.

I would also like to give thanks to the Veterans Foundation for their continued support of me and charities around our Country.
Now, I would be remiss if I did not thank our British heroes and those who have served for the HM Forces and those who continue to serve for our belated Queen and our new King.

Amber Guymer-Hosking

Charity Ambassador of Help4HomelessVeterans and a veteran of the British Armed forces, Amber served for 11 years before becoming medically discharged for PTSD in 2016 in turn.

Amber became homeless Living out of her car and in hotels before Help 4 Homeless Veterans helped her and her young son to get off the streets of the UK.

Since becoming an Ambassador to help other Veterans get their lives back on a stable path and support for their PTSD.

Amber has now become a stable shining light for many Veterans not only in the UK but Internationally by telling her story on Podcasts and in Magazines to help create awareness for the many of the Veterans that are still to this day living on our streets or struggling to cope with life out of the armed forces.

Still suffering from the traumatic effects of PTSD Amber still feels the side effects of it all from time to time as it will never leave her.

The Veterans Poems is dedicated to those who are still out there feeling abandoned after serving their country and still suffering from the traumatic events they have witnessed in their time.

"Sometimes the battle is hard and sometimes I have nearly thrown my own towel in because I wanted the pain to stop, though when this happens I have my own heroes, my son, my siblings, and the support of the people around me. "
"They give me strength"
"Amber Guymer-Hosking"

A Look Inside The Minds Of Our Veterans

A Look Inside The Minds Of Our Veterans.

A look inside the mind of our surviving Military Veterans across the United Kingdom.
Perhaps you see their injuries, the missing leg, the scarred face, the grey hairs.

Perhaps you see the average man, and the average woman having zero idea they have served your belated Queen and your Country.
Perhaps you have no idea that the effects of war have left that average man, that average
woman broke.

Perhaps, you have no idea of the loud clacking of your car exhaust would cause a flashback,
you in their faces being over-friendly could cause some triggers in their mind and cause sensory overload and a PTSD attack.

That nightclub you would like your friend to come too… does not feel safe to your military veteran, there is too much noise, too many people, and too many chances for danger.

Or it may remind them of a busy street from Baghdad or Northern Ireland. Perhaps, you have
no idea they are struggling.

You may think your friend is being rude when they say no, or shut off entirely, maybe, all they need is for you to understand and be patient with them.

Perhaps your husband or wife is having an outburst: being too emotional, too needy, too aggressive, too reserved, or they feel as though a massive elephant is sitting on their chest.

Perhaps they feel like they are suffocating. Perhaps they feel like their skin is crawling, perhaps they feel like their head is being shoved underwater.

Your Veteran wants to remove that elephant but they can't physically remove it on their own! they are generally screaming out for your support.

The elephant is getting heavier and it's crushing them, ''will you please help me move this elephant'' their ribs, heart, and chest is being squished, ''why can't you see the elephant?'

''Please, can you help me remove this elephant!'' ''Please be here for me''..'' I physically can't remove this elephant on my own.''

They need you to help them move the elephant off their chest!

Could you move an elephant off your chest alone?

It takes more than one person to move that elephant!

Support and your strength are needed.
Your Veterans' strength is being squished.

''I'm sorry I do not have the strength to do this alone,

I am sorry I need yours and I am making you tired too''

oh, they do feel like a burden to you, they feel in the way.

Yes, even without your help the elephant will soon want to move and the anxiety and pressure pass through your veteran is left bruised, exhausted, and tired.

And there certainly will be another elephant to come along for another quick rest!

For anxiety to come back around and sit on your veteran's chest.

Now the cycle repeats!

Though, the next time, the next time this elephant seems heavier than the one before.

crushing further down… is this because he or she is already bruised?

They haven't had enough time to heal or recover from the elephant before.

Please help your veteran remove that elephant in their chest.

Please help them recover so they are strong enough to handle the next one and please as a veterans partner, please do take some rest and recovery for you too.

You also do not want to get sat on by the elephant!

You also are important.

If you are a family member or a friend of a veteran who is suffering - please reach out to charities for support.

You are not alone!

If you see your veteran feeling suffocated or acting out of character please talk to them.

Please understand your normal, their old normal is now not normal.

That walk down a busy supermarket used to be a breeze, they were fine, happy, and content.

Still, on their good days they are still a breeze, but, on some days they are not, and some days that busy supermarket feels like the pits of hell.

they can't tell you which days!

They do not plan when it suddenly feels like hell.

It just happens.

You have to be prepared.

Today it could be a breeze for the first 30 minutes. then suddenly out of nowhere, they need to get out!

It's now hell.

Well, they were okay when they returned from war, they weren't Injured and they were making light of their stories!

That was a copying mechanism they were in survival the reality of war hadn't yet kicked in.

It could be anything!

We all know about the five sensors.

Sight, Sound, Smell, Taste, Touch,

Well PTSD is triggered by any one of these!

An episode of PTSD can be caused by any of the five senses.

No, your veteran will not always know or be sure of what triggered them.

They may not even understand what's happening to them.

They may not realize they have PTSD!

But now one of those senses has activated a memory, an unhealed wound, the band-aid well
that just got ripped off, and now the wound you do not see, the wound inside their mind is bleeding.

One of those senses just ripped open that wound... you can't see it, you just see your veteran acting out of character.

Yet, they are internally bleeding!

Their mind is now catastrophic, their mind un-easy, and having no idea what is happening to them!

They are confused!

you are confused- no idea why. And they, your veteran. The same.

They are confused and have no idea why. They suddenly feel like they are in hell!

As much as you are confused and stressed so are they. Some wounds you see, and some wounds are Invisible!

She or he is the tough veteran, a stand-up man or guy. They returned home from war.

No physical scratches and they seemed happy when they returned, though something slightly different.

 Though, you could never put your finger on it. they may talk of the odd few incidents and laugh as if it was a joke and then suddenly years later, as you watch the light in their eyes fade, as you watch their sparkle disappear, and yet,

You have no idea why!

You see, PTSD isn't always immediate, it comes on suddenly for e.g. when your partner becomes a parent and there are memories of war; children of their enemies, or killing a child's father for their own lives!

Yes, that's the harsh/awful/painful reality!

And now.
well now, reality has kicked in.
Guilt has kicked in.
PTSD has kicked in.

It could be a sudden smell, that they seemed unphased about before and wow that smell has triggered something, something they thought they long forgot!

It was never forgotten it was tucked down deep Inside their mind and now it's at the front!

It could be a date.. an anniversary of their colleague's passing.

Why are they here again?

Why are they at war again?

Why do they feel like they are surviving again? All you see is your beloved veteran, the same face, perhaps, just a different expression.

Same person, perhaps just a different tone in their voice.

The same smile, perhaps looking slightly altered.

Same hobbies, perhaps they have suddenly lost interest?

Same laugh, perhaps seemingly fake. Same banter, perhaps seemingly dark. Same outgoing friend, perhaps, seeing them less than you did before.

Perhaps, your veteran is internally bleeding from memories that keep seeping through their skin, through their eyes, through their ears, and through their mind!

Perhaps, your veteran can not switch off from these memories that are drowning them!

The memories that haunt them whilst they sleep, that haunt them through their waking hour. Perhaps, your veteran is feeling scared and alone and trapped inside their memories.

Guilt-ridden by the life they couldn't save, the man, woman, or child they killed! Their friend, their brother or sister they couldn't protect.

Perhaps, your veteran is wishing they died on that battlefield, perhaps, your veteran wants the memories to stop and go back down.

Perhaps, your veteran Is tired of the torture pain and memories, and any sense that triggers them. Perhaps, you are tired too.

Perhaps they are filled with more guilt from the burden they feel they are putting on you.

And perhaps, our heroes, well they need a hero too!

Perhaps, you are that Friend, their wife their husband, their sister, their brother, their mother, their father.

Perhaps you are their hero?

Perhaps, you can be the veteran's hero?

How annoying is all the 'perhaps'- well that's like the mind repeating the same memory over and over)

You as family and friends have no idea how much you save our veterans' lives!

You save them over and over again!

You may not always feel like you listening/supporting makes you a hero, but you are.

You see your veteran as a hero but they, your veteran, see you as theirs.

Thank you to our veterans and thank you to those who support our veterans.

Thank you to our charities and our mental health teams that support our veterans.

You are all remembered.

<u>What is PTSD?</u>

What is PTSD?

Well PTSD - post-traumatic stress disorder!
A mental health condition that can occur immediately or years after a traumatic event and not just from war, you can also get complex PTSD you can experience more than one traumatic event which has affected you greatly!

Does PTSD ever go away: no is your answer, no it never goes away… however, with effective evidence-based treatment, symptoms can be managed well and can remain doormats for years, even decades.

And there is a possibility for triggers at any apparent moment!

But NO, it never goes away!

PTSD symptoms:

Flashbacks to a traumatic event, nightmares, feeling extremely anxious, difficulty sleeping, intrusive thoughts.

Intense distress, an inability to connect properly with others, feeling detached or estranged from other people, isolation; anger outbursts, emotional outbursts, feeling sadness, feeling fear, or anger.

Physical sensations such as trembling sweating and nausea.

Mood changes, irritability, loss of memory, struggling to find words that were there a minute ago, forgetfulness; lack of motivation, changes in thinking pattern, hyper vigilant not feeling safe at all: a sense of impending doom, immediate danger depression, destructive behaviors, and the worst suicidal thoughts and actual suicide. So we have some physical sides of PTSD

What does it feel like, physically?

Increased blood pressure and heart rate, fatigue, muscle tension, nausea, and joint pain. Headaches, back pain, and other types of pains.
PTSD is an anxiety disorder hence physical symptoms are similar to anxiety!
According to recent studies PTSD and emotional trauma can cause brain damage and physical damage.
PTSD does affect your sleep.
Perhaps struggling to fall asleep is restless insomnia and nightmares- a lack of sleep affects your daily living!

Ptsd can create memory loss as well as an impaired ability to learn new things what can trigger an episode attack of PTSD?

Stressful situations can trigger an attack If PTSD, a relationship break downs-feeling similar emotions, arguing, fighting, seeing things that remind you of the event, for e.g.

You were in a car crash in a red car a year later you see a car the same color and same make as the car you were in an accident in this could trigger a PTSD attack.

Smelling something that reminds you of this event.

The five senses!

If any of those are activated and reminded of the event it can trigger a PTSD attack.

When you encounter this trigger you will go through some of the symptoms above and you could end up having a panic attack or bursting into violence or aggression and perhaps turn to a substance to ease the pain.

This could turn into self-harming through substance abuse, eating disorders, cutting yourself, or in another damaging activity.

How to help someone with PTSD?

Be patient

Be supportive as those with PTSD are more likely to experience social isolation, and avoid family and friends.

The sense of isolation can sometimes worsen the symptoms practice being a steady and reliable and trustworthy person In their lives.. do not push them when they are not ready.

Listen
Do not judge
Show respect

Learn about their triggers and what PTSD is not all symptoms are what you may see in the movies, some are less subtle and you may just think your friend is just quieter than usual when they could be having a start of a PTSD attack, notice the little things like a slight shift in their behaviors or sound of their t voices.

Help them seek out help and encourage them too.
Learn about PTSD so you can understand more
and make sure you have support too, learned to find ways for you to cope as their
support
the system you need to be okay too!
That's important.
What should you NOT say to someone with PTSD?

Just get over it they would if they could and they can't do not undermine their
feelings and what they are going through it's ten times what they are actually
showing!
Do not belittle them like that, instead support them!

"People have been through worse"
"You're overreacting"
'But that was a long time ago"
"Things weren't that bad"
"My friend went through something similar and she
got over it"
"You're too sensitive"
"You just have to face your fears"

And many other belittling things you could say to undermine their feelings and make
them feel even more useless than they already feel.
There could even be trigger words that trigger them into an attack, try and find out
what words trigger them.

Also be aware a lot of people like to blame everything on the person with PTSD oh
it's your PTSD when in fact they may actually be reacting to a normal situation like a
normal person, please do not gaslight someone with PTSD.

Remember they are not stupid, they are intelligent men and women have respect for
them!

Do not use their mental health disorder as an ex-issue to abuse them!
So now we have some facts about homelessness and PTSD.
Which is in turn why I am writing this short book.

<u>Amber Guymer-Hosking.</u>

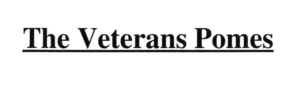

The Veterans Pomes

Our Veterans Poems

As Our thoughts wonder,
With heroes that fell,
And their families at home,
With stories to tell,

We fall silent on this day,
To remember them all,
The day young men died,
But our country stood tall,

The loss of so many,
That was hardly full grown,
Paid the ultimate price,
Fighting for home,

The echo of gunfire,
Hangs in the air,
When bravery turns futile,
And hope to despair,

Bodies like pebbles,
Cover the sand,
With photos of loved ones,
Clutched in their hands,

Comrades fight on,
While their colleagues lay
dead, The sea glowed pink.
And the rivers run red,

Churchill first spoke,
Of blood sweat and toil,
But who thought that so many, Would lay
dead on home soil?

Children in bed,
Writing letters of love,
Whilst air raids and bomb shells, Litter the
skies up above.

Telegrams of bad tidings,
Wives and mothers ask why?
Frightened soldiers in trenches, Trying
hard not to cry.

We are proud of our heroes,
Who paid the ultimate cost, Although we've
won wars,
Many battles we've lost.

So we stand here In silence,
Tall, proud, and bold, Remembering lost
souls,
That never grew old.

We feel a debt,
As our heads hang In sorrow, Because for
today,
They gave them tomorrow.

Written by Ian Thompson

Rego

An explosion,
A dream,
A nightmare,
A scream,
Emotionally Scarred,
By things that we've seen,

A young man,
A teen,
A soldier,
The scene,
A 19-year-old cog,
In this military Machine,

The noises,
The silence,
A commanders,

Guidance,
From shaking kids' hands,
To some uncontrolled
violence,

The villages,
The locals,
Misunderstood
Vocals,
Brewing their chai
For their mid-morning
Social's.

The mountains,
The heat,
The aching
If the feet,
Fatigue is advancing,
But we don't retreat,

We're Para's
Marines,
Fucking
Machines,
Always advancing, Through cloudy Smokescreens,

The contact,
A fight,
Lasting
All night,
The enemies tiring,
But we'll be all right,

A body,
Another,
A soldier,
His brother,

Took one to the chest, Whilst running for cover,

The sergeant
Calling,
The sunrise,
The fallen,
Time passes so soon, You struggle to recall,

The questions,
From friends,
The serving,
It ends,
He may appear normal, But a soldier pretends,

Emotional,
Scars,

New flashy
Cars,
Drowning his sorrows,
In nightclubs and bars,

A smile,
A joke,
Entertaining
The folk,
Not sharing emotions
Whenever he spoke,

A tough man,
But weak,
His outlook,
Is bleak,
Is it orders, comrades
Or a thrill that you seek,

The longing
Attraction,
To be in action,
Creeps in on occasion,
That you've moved on a fraction,

It's over,
Moving on,
Now them days,
Are gone,
It's a young man's career pal, And you're thirty one.

<u>Written by Anonymous 'One of the Para's</u>

<u>WE</u>

For once a year, they come out of their box.
Those dusty memories we hold aloft.
We stick out our chest, and down a port,
For those that we have lost.

We March with pride, with medals, shining.
And the last post plays its lonely tune.
Whilst we quietly shed a tear, for those we've lost.

We smile, and we sing.
We laugh. We joke.
But the pain we hide with laughter.
Whilst those that went before us,
Beam with pride.

At the close of the day, we raise a glass,
To our friends, our foes, and our brothers.
For we all are as one.

Whilst hiding feelings that make us who we are. To put on that
uniform,
Was a start to us becoming brothers and friends. Taking a vow to honor
and defend

To get together once a year,
And raise a glass and send good cheer.
To honour them is a must.
In service to god and country,
We put our trust.
As time goes by, year by year.
We must remember,
It's okay to shed a tear.
Lest we forget.

<u>Written by Matt Cole.</u>

A poem in memory of Queen Elizabeth ll.

This poem is for you, your majesty.

Flowers are laid, by your beloved nation.
To remember the queen of our generation.
We have our own memories of how you reigned,
Your true grit, understanding, and duty are sustained.

Your smile is admired all over the world,
Your kind words and wisdom, or experiences told.

Your empire adored you,
Your paintings hang proudly all over the world.
Where your commonwealth bowed.

Jubilee parties, celebrations, and fizz.
Commemorated your seventy years as our Liz.
No other monarch will reach that great height.
Of leading a nation.

Thank you.
Sleep tight.

Written by Matt Slater.

Friendly Fire

Friendly fire, what a quizzical term, Crouched there with your buddies,
By the perimeter berm.

Your weapons clean, you're ammo's dry, And friendly fire is the way
you die.
The reasons you went there,
Are varied I'm sure.

The duty-bound honor,
Was there to ensure,
You would be protected,
By the man at your back,
And you had this,
Against enemy attack

In your squad you had confidence,
In your country your love,
When friendly fire,
Rained down from above.
You lay for a moment, Disbelief sinking In, Along with reality,
And burning skin
The screams of the wounded,
You rolled to your side,
And as hard as you tried,
You couldn't stop the rolling tears,
That came from your eye.

For brothers in arms,
All right the fear,
Of friendly fire,
Year after year,

For the creed among soldiers,
Amidst death smells so putrid,
Is no fear of dying, but dying is stupid x

Well, it's not your fault brave warrior fair,
You and your courage,

Will always be there,
In the form of a gleaming white enduring light, That guides all brave
soldiers,
As they catch their last flight.
The contradiction "friendly fire"
Will continue to stand,
As you soar like an eagle,
To the promised land.

Written by Daniel Tweedy

It's OK

It's OK to cry.
Except when it's not.
When you're on tour and you're busy,
When you're prepping,
When you're traveling,
When you're arriving and handing over,
When you're flat out,
When you're tired and crawl into bed.
Somewhere in the crack of all this, emotion lies, waiting.

It's OK to be overwhelmed.
Except when it's not.
When your oppo needs you,
When your boss has a new objective,
When you need to focus,
When you're on the range,
When you're squeezing in a meal,
When you're tired and crawl into bed.
Somewhere in the crack of all this, emotion lies, waiting.

It's OK to lose hope.
Except when it's not.
When you're the one the new guy looks at for leadership,
When you're months away from R&R,
When you know it bleeds into everyone else,
When you just can't stop,
When you have a job to do,
When you're tired and crawl into bed.
Somewhere in the crack of all this, emotion lies, waiting.

So we wait.
We don't cry,
We fight being overwhelmed,
We don't lose hope.
Until we do, and then what?

Where's the support?
Where's the patience, the understanding, and the space to breathe?

Then it's over.
I'm a civvy now, and all there is time. Time to cry,
Time to be overwhelmed,
Time to lose hope.

We find a new focus,
We find new purposes,
We find ourselves.
Have patience with us.

It will take time to understand us.
It'll take time for us to breathe.
Just breathe.

It's OK

Written by Paul Rhodes

Maroon Kajaki

Through the darkness of the night
He patrols across the dead ground
Watching his footing and brothers
Trying not to make a sound.
The morning breaks as the birds sing
He lies in the cool low sun
He watches and scans
Waiting for his enemy to come.
Hours pass him by with only his gun
He lies with his brothers but feels so alone
His mind starts to remember
The sweet sights of home.

The silence is shattered
By a whip and a crack
For this, he has waited years
To unleash hell back.
His focus quickly sharpens
As he brings the gun into the aim
His clothes were soaked with sweat
Realizes this isn't a game.
As he opens up the General
With its distinguishing thud
He looks for his strike
In the compounds of mud.

After destroying his target
His job is nearly complete
He faces the long walk back
Relishing the chance for something to eat.
After cleaning the gun, on his bed, he lay
Mind wondering again about his day
And with a smile on his face
Was even more proud to wear his Maroon Beret.

Written by Glenn McAllister

Gwell Angau Na Chywilydd

Combination of me and my brother.
You don't know what I'm feeling,
Sat Inside this place,
Looking in the mirror,
Just to see a lonely face.

Looking for an opening,
To prove that you were right,
That you've joined the British Army,
And for your country, you will fight.

I could cope with all the physical,
But mental health took its course,
So I had to leave the army,
With emotions so remorse,

So when I look at all the things I've done, And places I've been.
There's just one motto,
That sticks in my mind,
Which has to be ich dien.

Death rather than dishonor,
That's what a Welshman says.
Gwell Angau Na Chywilydd,
Is what it means In wales

Written by Andrew Franklin

Only a soldier knows

They came from far and wide, Different towns, cities,
four countries United as one,
Only a soldier knows.

They all tell a different story,
Of why they joined,
But now with a bond,
They serve as one.
Only a soldier knows.

Months pass and years never happen, But we remember,
As only a soldier knows.

Friendships gained,
That last a lifetime,
Laugh and humor shared,
As only a soldier knows.

Foreign waters await the few,
Most return,
Few don't.
Only a soldier knows.

Tears abreast together,
Tears of pride, and honor, but tears, To say he was my friend.
Only a soldier knows.

And what awaits the rest,
Most return,
Few don't as we remember them, As only a soldier knows.

Written by Darren Devlin

They all tell a different story

A thousand battles - won or lost?
Deep regrets - who bear the cross?
A life fulfilled or a life denied?
No questions were answered with unchecked pride.

In the wilderness of a ravaged heart:
Fair forest flowers gently weep,
As wildcat growls for a soul to keep,
The footsteps of hope follow a gilded path.

They all tell a different story,
Of why they joined,
But now with a bond,
They serve as one.
Only a soldier knows.

We search for answers earthly from other souls,
While yet most wander blindly after future goals,
We search for answers spiritually from high above,
Only knowing at the very last truth originates from love.

Written by Nicky Davies

As day turns to dusk

As day turns to dusk,
Greying skies, rusting structures,
Cracked streets.
All welcome the shadows of darkness,
To hide their lost grace.
Not see the weeping heart.
The night serves only to enhance
Fears and magnify pains,
Light and warmth,
Are the antidote to grief's venomous grasp.

The world seems filled with private battles, Miniature conflicts of the
heart and soul,
Which echo
Like angry voices from empty walls.
Some say that kindness Is a weakness,
Some say that love is a faith of fools,
Truth says, that life without love means nothing.

When the flesh grows tired of the wind and the rain, When the mind Is
fatigued from stress and pain, What is left But the memory of love?

A life flies through years of time,
Punctuated by the turbulence of change,
Love is the air of life
Without which the journey could not begin,

My day starts and ends with love for you,
The sun rises and sets in your eyes.
My journey begins and ends in you're armed.

Written by Nicky Davies

Memories

When you've tasted the flavor of war, Something changes forever
more,
No matter what you ever do,
The haunting always stays with you.

Something triggers the memories,
And plagues you like a swarm of bees, A smell, a sound, sometimes
just a word, Can turn the reality of your world.

Nothing will ever be the same,
Because of that awful game,
Pyrotechnics simulate rifle fire,
And once again you're in the mire.

Rapid detonations and flashes you see, Just like a barrage of artillery,
Or someone who shouts in your face, Puts you back in that terrible
place.

Civilians can never understand,
Those who've seen a war-torn land,
No visible wounds of any kind,
But terrible scars within the mind.

Night time disturbed by dreams,
Of fallen wounded terrible screams, Mangled bodies blood and gore,
In memory of what you've seen before.

They are the victims of battle life, Suffering forever with battle strife,
So spare a thought before you mock,
It's no picnic this battlefield shock.

Written by Carl Coleman

Death in her eyes

I saw you on the news, Spouting your
political views, Twin towers,
Rubble showers.

You sent my daughter,
Their son,
To Afghanistan,
Chinook and gun.

Blue on blue,
Blood is red,
East Anglian offspring,
Now are dead.

Tend and mend,
Medic girl tries,
To treat the injured,
Death in her eyes

Written by Sarah Guymer

Do you even know

Do you even know what's inside my head?
It isn't just monsters under my bed,
I see your face,
We were on the chase,
The enemy is drawing in,
This is my war story, where do I begin?

Helmets and body armor on, guns in our hands,
We are on, foreign lands,
We take one step forward, careful where our feet lands, Hoping the
ground beneath us doesn't go bang,
We have our spacing,
We watch our tracing,
But honestly,
Most of us, don't even know what we are facing.
The first round fired,
Realizing we are not playing games,
Our country,
We were hired,
But we are the ones left in pain.

All I hear is rounds past my head,
I really wish I was tucked up in my bed,
Some go to war just as teens,
Though, we return feeling mean.
We witnessed things we cannot describe,
Our minds are now tortured,
Wishing we could click unsubscribe.
Our minds are constantly on replay,
Although for some, there is a delay,
We are home, but we are not safe,
Sweating. Trembling, angry, alone, misplaced,
We have triggers,
But now just a number in our nation's figures.

We need kindness and support,
Because for some, our war is constantly being fought, I see your dying
eyes,
Every time, like a goddam surprise,
Your blood, on my hands,
Along with the sound of your screams,
That I cannot stand.

This is on replay,
Why did you not stay,
It should have been me,
No, I do not want all of the glee,
You are the true hero here,
For me, every day I am left with fear.
One bang, one smell, one touch, takes me back again, I am done with
playing pretend,
I wish I was dead,
To stop this constant pain,
But for now,
I must, somehow, remain.

PTSD is not for the weak,
Even if sometimes, I do not speak,
It is easier to hide,
Though, I have sometimes lied,
I told you - I was fine,
Truth is, I feel like I committed a crime.
My body feels the repercussion,
To you all.
It looks like nothing.
I get mad and sad, I am so frustrated,
I wish I could say, this is overrated.
I cannot take back what has already been done,

Lives I could not save,

My mind is overrun,

My boots on with my comrades is all I know,

Brother, Sister I know I'm not alone,

My hero left on foreign lands,

Lying dead in dusty sands,

Even if I do not moan,

I will hold onto the grasp of your hands.

I raise a port,

You hero, are my first thought,

I drink to you, brother,

I will do my best,

Because we,

We will always share our memories of our bulletproof vest. We will remember them.

<u>Written by Amber Guymer-Hosking</u>

Maybe Tomorrow

It's a bling and a totter, down the lights of the high street, drunk by the train journey there.
Cackles and shouts, tales of shagging and swearing, and cosmetics squeeze out of the air.
Bravado and vanity, beer and wine, heading for the first open club,
Boys strut with their chests out, showing a leg, only thoughts are of getting a rub.

He's crouched in the corner, a top of a damp box, wrapped in a half-soaking doss bag, A dog by his side, as companion and protector, a mucker to share a sparse nose bag
He shakes with the cold, but also the comedown,
The cider has long since left him.

A blot-out, a release, from the pain in his mind and the mess he now finds himself in.

The thoughts flood his senses, and the reality hits home, he's back in a freezing cold street, His weakness is bared for all to see and the clubbers throw contempt at their feet,
He no longer begs, for his pride has been shattered, his bones took a battering too,

''Fucking Alcy old tramp! Get a job!''
''I don't work to pay your special brew''
No safe place left, for he was banned from the hostel, the drink made dam sure of that, He Lost control of his bowels, soon followed his patience, and they took back the key to his flat,
It wasn't so bad, a few months ago
His life going back the right way.
But his pride took a knock, as often it had
Frosty jack led him back to today.

He lays in the street, in a terrible mess, and the clubbers sneer or ignore him

It's all his own fault, he chose a life of addiction, as opposed to what lay before him This is true in a way, as a harsh fact of life, but the soapbox is on shaky ground
For he once had perfect control of his life, a young family, and a wife around.

He thinks of them now in his darkest moments, they even cut through the jade
He loves them dearly and it tears at his soul, they won't hold his touch or his gaze

See, a soldier once, and proud he was too, professional, dedicated, and bright
Filled with compassion and a guardian of others
Till the flash and the bang of that night

He still hears the silence, can still feel the heat, taste the coppery stench of the gore.

Intact and undamaged, but his muckers around him, a crimson display on the floor!
The dust in his eyes, that warm sickly wetness, the smell you cannot explain
The feels emptiness and ultimate guilt as he stands in a crouch filled with pain.

The guilt never left him, nor thoughts of that day, but talking about it was never an option
So he bottled it up, pushed everyone away, and slowly put his life up for adoption.
But the booze killed the voices, the smells, and the guilt only for a while in the doss bag.
His fault for not being idle, nor being self-centered, he wanted to be strong for others. His fault was pride and misplaced guilt, as he watched the death of his brothers.
The callous jeers and judging stares, of the passers-by this Saturday night

Steel his resolve, for what he must do. It's time to make things right.
The ciders have worn off, but there are pills in his pocket, he saved
them for a while

The twenty should do it and no one notice Just another dead tramp in a
pile
He holds back a tear, the shaking more violent, he feels sick to the
core of his soul.
A spinning mass of vivid recollection filled his mind like a bowl.

He didn't notice her as she approached, too wrapped in what he must
do
She crouched by his side, this total stranger, and asked ''hi, How are
you''
Bewildered and shocked, he took in her features and muttered.
''OK, thanks"
"And you''

They spoke for ten minutes, and she brought him back a coffee, and a
warm box of chips from the van Spoke to him as an equal, just down
on his luck, and made him remember the man

When she left, he felt better Though somehow the same, got the pills
and the dregs of his brew
''Maybe tomorrow'' he thought to himself.

<u>Written by Kev Walker</u>

An Afghan Christmas.

Prepared for the heat; Surprised by the cold; Christmas in Afghan;
At 19 years old;

My sisters at home;
Brothers by my side; Excited and nervous;
But oozing with pride;

A shoebox of goodies; Deodorant and socks;
Some family photos;
A selection box;

A moment reflecting;
What time is it there?
My niece has grown bigger; Look at all of that hair;

I laugh at a thought;
While I stare at the floor; I've never really cared; About Christmas
before;

But this time it's different; No family meeting;
No game of monopoly; With somebody cheating;

No face full of nibbles;
Or my favorite thing;
Eating myself sick;

With a full prawn ring;

As much as they miss me; I'm sure they'll be fine; They'll probably
toast me; With their beers and wine;

While you're pulling your crackers; Pull one for me;
A song about partridges;
In a pear tree;

The mess hall is ready;
It's time for some scoffing;
We all trundle around;
Like sheep in a trough;
Surprised by the spread;
And the Christmas décor;
I've never seen anything;
Quite like it before;

The smiles on faces;
The hugs and high fives;
Officers singing;
And hideous jives;

Unexpectedly awesome;
This turned out all right;
I picked 5 extra sprouts;
For the pending food fight;

A minute of chaos;
My hair full of mash;
I had the most fun I've had; Without spending cash;

I pocket some turkey;
To feed the camp stray;
I sit down and stroke her;
She's chomping away;
Does she know it's Christmas? Who cares if she's been fed;
Head back to the cabin;
To FaceTime in bed;

The blurred family faces; There's a bad signal
here;
A glimpse of grandad;
Holding his beer;

It all looks in order;
A standard affair;
My niece with her face;
Full of chocolate eclair;

Comparing our stories;
My uncle Phil's sweater;
Their Christmas looks fun;
But I think mine was better;

Food fight with the brass;
Mess walls full of trifle;
Early night with hot chocolate; Snuggled next to
my rifle;

Festivities over;
Let work recommence;
It's my turn to stay on;
And take care of defense;

I stare at the darkness;
As the snow starts to fall;
Merry Christmas back home; Merry Christmas
to all.

Written by Anonymous

Airborne

How many times have I cast my mind's eye down there deep into the
water?
Where we blindly seek images, sounds, and feelings reflected from the
pool of the past. A place where memories are blurred and thoughts are
fractured.
Yet memories can dart into the brain as keen and pellucid as diamond
needles,
As though a memory possessed a will of its own, unfathomable to human
understanding.
Are we simply tormented by the spirits who witness our loss and our
weakness?
Forced to gaze bright-eyed at the clarity of failure and unable to reclaim
the glory of heady success.
Still deeper, past the tentacle weeds of hesitation and confusion,
Navigating powerful currents of fear, anger, and sadness,
I search the very sand bed of my life for a source of light.

A torch that I might shine upon the present and up beyond the clouds of
the future
A beam of brilliant emancipating truth guiding my destiny to something
certain, a
safer place.
As day turns to dusk
Greying skies, rusting structures, cracked streets
All welcome the shadows of darkness to hide their lost grace
Not so the weeping heart.
The night serves only to enhance fears and magnify pains
Light and warmth are the antidotes to grief's venomous grasp

The world seems filled with private battles.
Miniature conflicts of the heart and soul echo
Like angry voices from empty walls
Some say that kindness is a weakness
Some say that love is the faith of fools
Truth says that life without love means nothing:

When the flesh grows tired of the wind and the rain
When the mind is fatigued from stress and pain
What is left but the memory of love?

A life flies through years of time
Punctuated by the turbulence of change
Love is the air of life without which the journey could not begin

My day starts and ends with love for you.
My sun rises and sets in your eyes.
My journey begins and ends in your arms.

You, whose spirit harbors the elements:
The grace of air, the beauty of water,
The passion of fire, The wisdom of wood,
And the strength of the metal.

Do not see us as a fading memory,
Do not hear our voices with sadness,
Do not speak of our love as dead.

Through those crystal clear coral eyes,
Sometimes I swear I could see your soul.
In my mind's eye our past flashes by,
As though comet dust in this lonely night sky.

All of these earthly notions, these spiritual dreams,
Falling gently into the carefree sleepy void
Lost like tears in the rain.

My heart is crying for my love
My love cannot hear my heart
My words are deaf and dumb
My heart cannot speak in words

Can you feel my shame?
Can you sense my pain?
Can you trust me again?
Can you forgive my blame?

Do not see us as a memory
Do not hear our voices as echoes from the past
Do not speak of our love as dead

There is still a light burning
It is weak and it is tired
Once it was burning brave and bright
Now it flickers like a candle on a sea of doubt

Please nurture this flame
My hearts' hope rests upon it
When you scc my eyes, you will see my heart
You will hear it and feel its warmth again

If your heart refuses to listen
If nothing can rekindle the fire
Then I will wait for you in silence my love
I will guard the flame until I hear your voice again

A thousand battles - won or lost?
Deep regrets - who bear the cross?
A life fulfilled or a life denied?
No questions were answered with unchecked pride.

In the wilderness of a ravaged heart:
Fair forest flowers gently weep,
As wildcat growls for a soul to keep,
The footsteps of hope follow a gilded path.

We search for answers earthly from other souls,
While yet most wander blindly after futile goals.
We search for answers spiritual from high above,
Only knowing at the very least: truth originates from love".

<u>Written by Nicky Davies</u>

Is that enemy fire effective?
It's landing nearby.
If we return fire,
We'll have to explain why.

Now that`s too close for comfort, "Contact front" bullets sprayed. A
puddle of claret,
On the floor where he laid.
You were close my old foe, Closer than the last.
And the ones before that,
That have tried in the past.

It's funny really,
Next week's R&R.
I'll remember this scene,
While I'm sitting in a bar.

Had your shots hit their target, And roles were reversed.
It could be you at the table, Quenching your thirst.
But the luck was with me,
In the prone on that mound.
3 thousand miles away,
At a bar, it's my round.

Il be back there next week,
In the heat and the dust.
One thing for certain,
Survival`s a must.

Watching their movement, Through green glowing eyes. Approaching
some village, Beneath moonlit skies.

The tinnitus ringing,
The visible breath.
Could today be my turn?
Not yet Mr death.

The silence deafens,
And hairs start to stand.
The senses are warning,
An ambush is planned.
The blast was impressive,
Hot shrapnel rained.
Some limbs were abandoned,
And prosthetics gained.
A night to remember,
I've tried to forget.
The dreams are immersive,
As real as they get.

But there's no time for sorrow And no room for stress.
The world keeps on turning, And we must progress.

Experience and memories, Locked away in your head. Come flooding
out sometimes, When lay in your bed.
But they don't define us,
They don't make us weak.
It takes real courage,
To stand up and speak.
To say "I am a soldier"
And sometimes I've cried. Blaming myself,
For the ones that have died.

When here I am living,
With time left to burn.
The occasional feeling, Wanting to return.
But il hold it together,
And never forget.
My journey from civvy,
To armed forces vet.

Written by Anonymous

'Battlefield Shock'

When you've tasted the flavor of war, Something changes forever
more,
No matter what you ever do,
The haunting always stays with you,

Something triggers the memories,
And plagues you like a swarm of bees,
A smell, A sound, or sometimes just a word, Can turn the reality of
your world,

Nothing will ever be the same,
Because of that awful game,
Pyrotechnics simulate rifle fire,
And once again you're in the mire,

Rapid detonations and flashes you see, Just like a barrage of artillery,
Or someone who shouts in your face,
Puts you back in that terrible place,

Civilians can never understand,
Those who've seen a war-torn land,
No visible wounds of any kind,
But terrible scars within the mind,

Night time disturbed by dreams,
Of fallen wounded terrible screams, Mangled bodies blood and gore,
In memory of what you've seen before,

They are the victims of battle life, Suffering forever with battle strife,
So spare a thought before you mock,
It's no picnic this battlefield shock.

Written by Carl Coleman

I Shake

The palate is thick and pungent.
Ripe yet rotten. Though rotting has not yet begun.
There are shades of urea, undertones of copper, and a hint of raw pork
in a pan.

Whilst in this state, the freshness shocks, indeed it almost smells tasty
This matter should stink, not hint at the taste buds, my skin hues
quickly to pasty.

The ringing was still clear, this taste in my lungs, a broken marionette
of gore
Doused in crimson and black, a stinkhorn mushroom, draped across
the sand on the floor.
The palate is so thick, it stays in my nostrils, and lies dormant for
years at a time
Till a familiar smell, dilutes and hydrates it waking hideous fears that
were mine.

Defenseless against it, it shadows my being, my stomach a churning
mass
Goosebumps for no reason and magnified senses, awaiting the gut
wrench to pass.

You can't fight or ignore it, it only adds to the
fear, the sickly strength of its grip
Fills your heart with blackness, loss, and frustration and exposes your
soul with a rip.
It sleeps when it chooses, not at my will, but sleeps to allow it to
wake
Refreshed and visceral, stronger than ever, my palms grip my face
and I shake.

Written by Kev Walker

Peace of mind

Peace of mind – an absence of anxiety.
How I long for the day self-hatred says goodbye to me.
You left me with nothing but pain.

A physical and mental scar of who you are and who I once was.
Gone.
Nothing.
Staring at my body, I saw what you saw and what I let you do.
I didn't let you do anything, but you chose to do it. And I hope you
find peace of mind knowing what you left behind.
Nothing.

Nothing but the shell of a broken woman. Flashback and emotions.
Sadness. Pain.
Jealousy?
I'm jealous of you, you see.
Of how you'll find peace of mind eventually.
Of how you can look in the mirror and be happy.
Me? How I wish to be empty. Just like the old me. I wish to be the old
me. I wish to be nothing. Because being nothing is better than being
what you've made me.

Unstable. I need to find balance.
A balance between then and now.
They say to put the past behind you, but you're back every night.
And every time I see myself, I want to cry, and they wonder why I hate
myself more than I hate you.
What I let you do.
They say I'm a fighter.
But I didn't fight.

Written by Charlotte Meakin

In memory of our Men and Woman
Who where left on the battlefield

We will remember you.

The reality of conflicts in Afghanistan.

We will remember you.

Operations in Afghanistan

This is the reality of how many soldiers we lost in one war zone on the battlefield.

This is not the list of those who have since committed suicide from their conflict in Afghanistan.

Over the last 20 years of deployment in Afghanistan, there have been 457 deaths of UK armed forces personnel. The number of fatalities peaked between 2009 and 2010 when over 100 personnel were killed. Of the total 457 personnel who died whilst on deployment to Afghanistan 405 died because of hostile action.

During Operation Herrick, the codename for which all British military operations were conducted from 2002 to 2014, there were 616 serious or very serious casualties among armed forces and civilian personnel. As with deaths, these casualties peaked in 2009 and 2010.

There were a total 7,807 field hospital admissions, although most admissions were related to disease or a non-battle injury. Around 28% (2,209) of admissions to field hospitals were those wounded in action.

Additionally, there were 7,477 medical air evacuations during the 12-year operation.

We will remember all of you who have lost your lives on the battlefield and the ones who lost their battle at home once returning from the battlefield.

Since 1945, the deadliest year for the British Armed forces was 1951, when there were 851 operational deaths. This was due to three separate conflicts: the Malayan Emergency, the 1951 Anglo-Egyptian War, and the Korean War. Between 1959 and 2009 there were only three years that had more than 100 operational deaths: 1972, 1973, and 1982. The spike in deaths in the early 1970s was the result of the political violence in Northern Ireland at the time, and 237 of the 297 deaths in 1982 happened during the Falklands War. Over this period there have been a total of 7,192 British military deaths in conflicts.

Who lost their lives on active duty for their Country and their Families.

We will remember you.

Over 145 thousand personnel in 2020
The British Armed Forces are composed of four separate branches, the British Army, the Royal Navy, the Royal Air Force, and the Royal Marines. Of these branches, the British Army has more personnel than the other three combined at over 82 thousand. The Royal Air Force had around 33 thousand personnel, the Navy at over 27 thousand, and the Marines at 6.64 thousand amounting to 145 thousand overall.

The Royal British Legion's long-held estimate is that somewhere between three and
six percent of homeless people have an armed forces background, but there are concerns that some homeless veterans are rendered "invisible" by the way statistics are collected.
In a 2014 report surveying the ex-forces community, the Legion reported that the number of veterans living on the streets in London has plummeted since the 1990s when figures indicated that 20 percent of the homeless population was ex-services at the time. A 2008 study found that the proportion had dropped to six percent.

More recent statistics suggest that rough sleeping among veterans is at an even lower rate in the present day. The Combined Homelessness and Information Network,
known as CHAIN, track the flow of rough sleeping in London and is regarded as one of the most accurate measures in the UK, ahead of the official annual counts.

The database revealed the percentage of UK nationals with experience serving in the armed forces was as low as three percent in 2017/18 and fell to two percent in 2018/19. And the percentage remained the same for 2019/20 with 129 UK veterans seen by outreach workers sleeping rough. When foreign nationals are taken into account, six percent of people sleeping rough in 2019/20 had served in the armed forces at some point in their lives.

But the London-centric nature of the figures demonstrates just one of the problems with counting how many veterans are homeless across England and the wider UK. In early 2020, the University of Salford academic Mark Wilding penned a report on the subject which found that veterans were "predominantly self-referring into direct access hostels or accessing support through Armed Forces charities and community organizations" rather than going through the statutory homelessness system.

The problem with the statistics the way that they are is it renders homeless veterans invisible.

This is backed up by statistics showing the number of veterans approaching councils for help with homelessness in England between April and June 2019. A total of 70,030 households were assessed and owed a prevention or relief duty – when the council is required to step in to prevent or relieve homelessness under the Homelessness Reduction Act – but only 440 were recorded as needing support due to serving in the armed forces, making up 0.63 percent of the figures.

While reporting to armed forces charities is not problematic in itself, with ex-servicemen and women able to access specialist support, Wilding suggested that some homeless veterans were being rendered "invisible" in statistics.

He said: "It shouldn't necessarily be the case that you have to go the statutory homelessness route because veterans often have special issues that the local authority homelessness team might not be best equipped to cope with this.

"It should be that they can get that support from armed forces charities, especially if they are best placed to help them, but this needs to be recognized. Because beyond the knowledge of these armed forces charities who are doing that work, it becomes quite separated from homelessness as a mainstream issue.

"The charities are doing that work but this is the problem with the statistics in the way that they are – it renders homeless veterans invisible."

Wilding insisted that there needs to be a change in how homelessness statistics are collected to improve coverage, suggesting that replicating the CHAIN model elsewhere would benefit how we understand not only rough sleeping but the scale of veterans living on the streets.

A greater take-up of the Armed Forces Covenant – a promise by the nation ensuring that those who serve or who have served in the armed forces, and their families, are treated fairly – among housing organizations could also help to join up the work being already done to combat homelessness among veterans.

The academic added: "It's pretty difficult to get to the crux of the problem. It would require the government to change the way that homelessness statistics are collected because they are based on priority needs. So in that sense, homelessness statistics are an underestimate of what's actually out there.

"There's definitely scope for bottom-up work to be done. The work that CHAIN does is supported by the London Mayor so perhaps if other regions were able to get that support from the local government then they could do similar things.

And help to try and get attention to the issue."

Conflicts of the
British Amy

1 Roman Invasion & Conquest (55 BC-96 AD)

·2 Viking & Anglo-Saxon Invasions (5th-10th Centuries)

·3 Norman Conquest & Subsequent Conflicts (1066-1071; 12th century)

·4 Barons' Wars (1215-1217; 1264-1267)

·5 Hundred Years' War(1337-1453)

·6 War of the Roses (1455-1487)

·7 Anglo-Spanish War (1585-1604)

·8 Wars of the Three Kingdoms (1639-1653)

·9 Seven Years' War

·10 The American Wars

·10.1 Queen Anne's War (1702-1713)
·10.2 War of the American Independence (1775-1783)
·10.3 War of 1812 (1812-1814

·11 Napoleonic Wars & Resulting Conflicts (1803-1815)
·11.1 Anglo-Russian War (1807-1812)
·11.2 Anglo-Swedish War (1810-1812)

12 Anglo-Afghan Wars (1839–1842; 1878–1880; 1919)
·13 Crimean War (1853–1856)

14 The Boer Wars (1880-1881; 1899-1902)

·15 The Great War (1914-1918)

·16 World War II (1939-1945)

·17 The Cold War (1947-1991

Northern Ireland,
First second and third Cod war
The troubles 1968-1998
Aden Emergency 1963-1967
Indonesia -Malaysia conflict 1963-1966
The Falklands,1982

Iraq,

Lebanon 1982-1984
The gulf war 1990-1991
Bosnian war
Operation desert fox
Kosovo war

Sierra Leone

Libyan war

Operation shader

Persian gulf crises

To Summarize

We have talked about the reality, the facts, and the feelings.. taken a look inside the minds of our veterans, and looked at some harsh realities.

This book has been created to spread awareness, to raise money towards Help4homeslessveterans

And to raise the knowledge of PTSD and Homelessness in the United Kingdom.

Please if you feel affected by anything in this book please ensure you reach out for
help or support and get support.

PTSD is not just for soldiers, civilians can get this too.

Please, everybody, think of one thing you like about yourself today. Think about one thing you achieved today.

Think about your dream/Goal.. and what would your first small task be to help achieve your dream?

Please find five minutes to just move your body around and step into the sunshine. Please create positivity and encourage others to be positive.
Namaste

Thank you for your support.

Kind regards.

Amber Guymer-Hosking

The Veterans Poems

Published By
Film Volt Group
2023
Company Number 11833932